INSPIRATIONS

Hartley on the Rocking Horse by Alice Neel.

INSPIRATIONS

Stories About Women Artists

Georgia O'Keeffe · Frida Kahlo
Alice Neel · Faith Ringgold

LESLIE SILLS

Albert Whitman & Company   Niles, Illinois

*For the children of the Children's Creative
Clay Studio School and for Eric.*

I am very grateful to all the people who encouraged and nourished this book.
Kathy Tucker, thank you for selecting my manuscript and believing in my ideas.
Ann Fay, your support, enthusiasm, wonderful suggestions, and kind ways have
spoiled me. Patricia Hills, Faith Ringgold, Bernice Speiser, Linda Gilbert-Schneider,
and Dr. Solomón Grimberg have all made enormous contributions. I appreciate
the cooperation of the people who lent photographs of the artists and their works,
particularly Nancy Neel and the rest of the Neel family, the Robert Miller Gallery,
the Bernice Steinbaum Gallery, and the Imogen Cunningham Trust. I want to thank
my husband, Robert Oresick, as well, for without his feminist consciousness and love,
none of this would have been possible.

Library of Congress Cataloging-in-Publication Data

Sills, Leslie.
   Inspirations: stories about women artists / Leslie Sills.
      p. cm.
   Summary: Discusses the lives and art of Frida Kahlo, Georgia
O'Keeffe, Alice Neel, and Faith Ringgold. Includes color
reproductions of their work.
   ISBN 0-8075-3649-0
   1. Women painters—United States—Biography—Juvenile literature.
2. Painting, American—Juvenile literature. 3. Painting,
Modern—20th century—United States—Juvenile literature. 4. Kahlo,
Frida—Juvenile literature. 5. Painters—Mexico—Biography—
Juvenile literature. 6. Painting, Mexican—Juvenile literature.
7. Painting, Modern—20th century—Mexico—Juvenile literature.
[1. Women artists. 2. Artists.] I. Title.
ND212.S47 1989
759.13—dc19
[B]   88-80
[920]   CIP
                                             AC

Text © 1989 by Leslie Sills.
Cover and interior design by Karen Yops.
Published in 1989 by Albert Whitman & Company,
5747 W. Howard, Niles, Illinois 60648.
Printed in U.S.A. All rights reserved.

10 9 8 7 6 5 4 3 2

CONTENTS

Georgia O'Keeffe

Georgia O'Keeffe in 1915,
when she was twenty-eight years old.

In 1887, on a farm outside of Sun Prairie, Wisconsin, a little girl was born into the family of Ida and Francis O'Keeffe. She was named Georgia Totto O'Keeffe after her mother's father, George Totto. Georgia was the second of seven children.

Even when she was little, Georgia was unusual. She was always extremely aware of her surroundings. As an adult, she could recall things she had seen when she was only a baby. She remembered being propped up among large pillows on a quilt outdoors in the bright sunshine. The pillows looked very white, and the quilt had two kinds of fabric, one with small red stars on a white background and the other with red and white flowers on a black background. A woman nearby was wearing a print dress with small blue flowers on it.

Georgia was an independent child with a mind of her own. If her sisters wore ribbons, she didn't want to wear them; if they wore their hair up, she wanted to wear hers down! Although she always had siblings to play with, she often preferred to play alone with her dolls. She enjoyed making doll clothes for them and devised a collapsible dollhouse that she could carry around on the farm.

Georgia spent a great deal of time outdoors when she was growing up. She enjoyed watching the changes of season and the growth cycle of the trees and flowers. Sometimes she walked through the fields with her father to check the progress of the crops. Nature—what she later called "the wideness and wonder of the sky and the world"—was an important part of her life.

When Georgia was about ten years old, her mother arranged for her and her sisters to take private drawing and painting lessons. In those days, art was considered a proper hobby for girls. Georgia especially enjoyed watercolor painting, but she grew tired of the lessons. Her teachers had her copy pictures while she preferred to do her own art experiments at home.

In one such experiment, she painted a lighthouse by the sea and in another, the winter night outside her bedroom window. In the lighthouse picture, she struggled to make the sun look bright. She found if she placed it against a cloudy sky, it seemed to shine brighter. The night picture was even more difficult. What color should she paint the snow, trees, and sky? Snow doesn't really look white in the

Blue and Green Music, 1919.

Jack-in-the-Pulpit I, 1943.

moonlight, but she thought it should be white. The trees looked black, but she thought they should be dark blue since it was night. Finally she found the right colors. She mixed dark blue with black for the trees and left the paper blank for the snow. She painted the sky lavender gray.

By the age of thirteen, Georgia knew she wanted to be an artist. She wasn't sure where she got the idea. Even though she had taken art lessons, she hadn't seen many professional paintings. There was a small drawing in one of her mother's books that she thought was beautiful, though. It was of a girl and was called the *Maid of Athens.* Perhaps it started Georgia thinking about becoming an artist.

All through high school, Georgia had art lessons, but sometimes they were not so helpful. Once, a teacher criticized a drawing so harshly that Georgia felt like crying. The teacher said that the lines were too black and the form too small. She even drew over Georgia's picture! Georgia felt terrible but still thought her drawing was more beautiful than the teacher's.

Fortunately, she had some good lessons, too. One was a class about the jack-in-the-pulpit, a spring wildflower. The teacher pointed out the different parts and colors of the flower. This lesson made Georgia look closely at details and started her thinking about painting something alive. When Georgia became an adult, she painted six pictures of the jack-in-the-pulpit.

Her last two years of high school were spent at Chatham Episcopal Institute in Virginia. There she was different from the more traditionally feminine Southern girls, who wore frilly dresses and tended to be flirtatious. Georgia liked to dress very plainly and was reserved around boys. She was well liked, though, maybe because she was full of mischief. She drew funny pictures of the teachers and sometimes got in trouble for staying up too late or going for walks in the country. Luckily she had a teacher who recognized her artistic skills and encouraged her in spite of her mischievous ways. Her watercolor of red and yellow corn won the Chatham art prize.

During her college years, Georgia first went to the Art Institute of Chicago and then to the Art Students' League in New York City. She enjoyed her classes but something was missing for her. Even though she did well and won a scholarship for a prize still life, she felt her work was only what her teachers wanted. She longed to paint what was important to *her,* even if she wasn't sure what that was yet.

Then one night when she was walking along the Hudson River, she saw something that she could not forget. In the night sky were two poplar trees

creating a beautiful pattern. When Georgia returned home, she tried to paint what she had seen. Doing that felt better than all her lessons.

Georgia had planned to stay in New York City to continue her studies, but her family was having financial problems and could no longer afford to send her to school. She returned to Chicago to live with relatives and take an advertising job drawing embroidery and lace.

After two years, though, Georgia came down with the measles and was forced to join her family in Virginia, where they now lived. The illness had temporarily weakened her eyes, making it impossible for her to continue such demanding work. When she was well enough, her sister encouraged her to attend a painting class at the University of Virginia. Fortunately she did and there met a teacher named Alon Bement. Bement spoke about art in a way Georgia had never heard before. He told his students that it is most important to fill a space in a beautiful way. To Georgia this idea seemed "of use to everyone—whether you think of it consciously or not. . . . Where you have the windows and doors in a house. How you address a letter and put on the stamp. What shoes you choose and how you comb your hair." Bement gave his students exercises to do with different shapes and encouraged them to create their own designs. He spoke about shades of color and flowing lines as a way to express feelings. He even played music in his classes for his students to express visually. Georgia felt Bement was giving her an "alphabet," equipment to work with so that she could make art a thing of her own.

Bement had learned these ideas from his teacher, Arthur Wesley Dow, a professor at Columbia University Teachers College in New York City. Georgia was eager to study with Dow. To earn enough money, she worked for the next two years as an art supervisor and teacher in the Amarillo, Texas, public schools. Then she returned to New York City to take Dow's classes.

Her work with Dow was stimulating, but she was again frustrated. Her feelings were too strong to be expressed in his simple art exercises.

In the fall of 1915, Georgia took a position teaching art at a Methodist women's college in South Carolina. While she did not want to leave New York City, she knew this job would allow her time to do her own work. She would be able to isolate herself and examine her past efforts.

As Georgia looked over the work she had done, each painting still seemed the result of what one teacher or another had wanted her to do. She said to herself, "I have things in my head that are not like

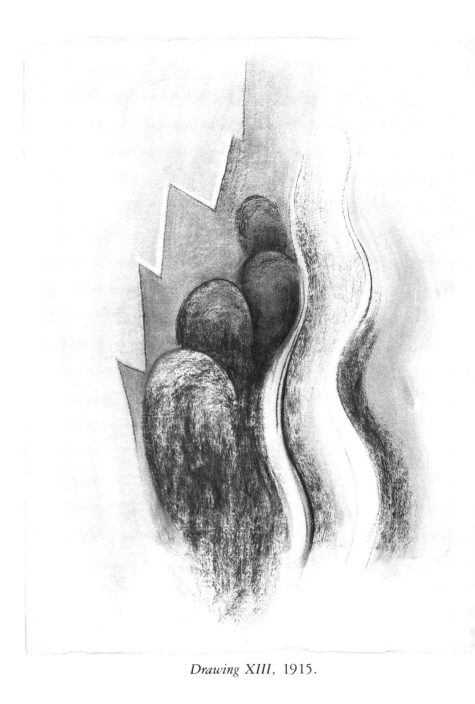

Drawing XIII, 1915.

what anyone has taught me—shapes and ideas so near to me—so natural to my way of being and thinking that it hasn't occurred to me to put them down." Georgia put away her old paintings and began again, drawing the shapes that she saw in her mind.

Her *Drawing XIII* was done during this period. She worked in black and white and would not allow herself to use color. The pictures were not of recognizable subjects like trees or flowers. They were abstractions—lines and shapes created with tones, different shades of black and white—all expressing her emotions.

Georgia was so pleased with her new work that she sent it to her friend Anita Pollitzer for her comments. Anita was her closest friend from her school days in New York. They often discussed their art ideas and the work of other artists. Georgia told Anita not to show these drawings to anyone, but Anita thought there was one person who must see them—Alfred Stieglitz.

Mr. Stieglitz was a powerful man in the New York art world. He was a gifted photographer who also owned an art gallery called 291 where he showed some of the newest, most talked-about artwork in America and Europe.

Stieglitz loved Georgia's drawings immediately. In fact, he hung them on his gallery walls, but he did not ask her permission. Because Georgia was again in New York studying with Dow, she quickly found out. She was furious at first and went to the gallery to have them removed. Stieglitz, however, convinced her to leave them up. Georgia and he talked and soon realized they had a lot to share.

To support herself, Georgia had to leave New York to take a job as teacher and head of the art department at West Texas State Normal School in Canyon, Texas. While she had many responsibilities, she managed to paint a great deal. She also carried on a lively correspondence with Stieglitz, sharing her thoughts and feelings.

Georgia was inspired by Texas, particularly the vast plains that went on and on like the ocean. Often she and her sister Claudia, who was living with her, took long walks outside of Canyon to watch the sunsets. With such a colorful world around her, Georgia now really wanted to put color back in her work.

Evening Star III is one of a series of ten paintings. It shows the joy she felt in her Texas setting and her fascination with the brightness of the evening star and the constantly changing sky around it.

Unlike *Drawing XIII, Evening Star III* is about something recognizable, but it is similar to Georgia's abstractions. She simplified what she saw into a few

Evening Star III, 1917.

horizontal and swirling lines and a few colors. If we did not see the title, we might think that the work *was* an abstraction. Georgia often painted what she saw in nature, but she didn't believe in copying. She tried to simplify, to get at the heart of things. She believed this was the best way to explain her feelings about nature.

Watercolor was the perfect medium for her to use for her Canyon paintings. As a busy teacher, she didn't have time to work in oil paints, which dry slowly. With watercolors, she could quickly capture the rapidly changing light. By adding water to the paints and painting one thin layer of color over another, she could create the effect of light shining in the sky.

Another watercolor from this period is *Light Coming on the Plains II*. Again, she has painted something recognizable—early morning on the plains right before dawn—but she has simplified it into an egg shape using different shades of a single color. Georgia left spots of paper bare in between the bottom of the painting and the domed top to give the effect of sparkling light.

After almost two years in Canyon, Georgia gave up teaching and moved back to New York City to paint full-time and to be with Stieglitz. After six years, she and Stieglitz married.

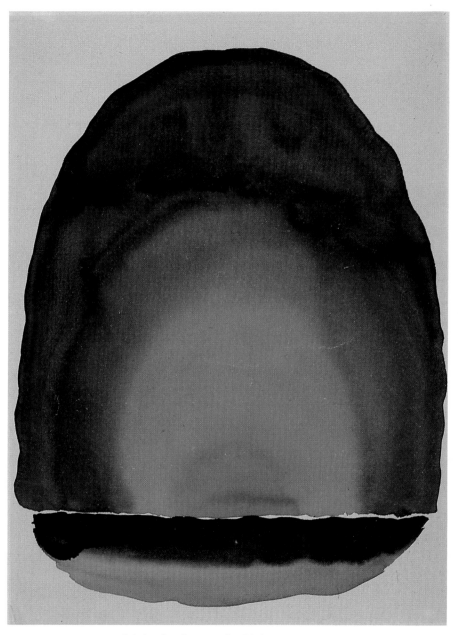

Light Coming on the Plains II, 1917.

Stieglitz took hundreds of photographs of Georgia. Sometimes he would photograph just her hands or her head and neck. Georgia said that seeing these photographs helped her to understand herself better and so helped her as an artist. Stieglitz helped Georgia in another way, too. He showed her work in his gallery year after year. With every showing the newspapers wrote lovingly about her paintings, and almost from her first exhibition, they sold for high prices.

As Georgia continued to work, she sometimes painted recognizable subjects and sometimes did not. *Blue and Green Music* doesn't look like something we could name. It is a pure abstraction that shows Georgia's strong feelings for music. Like *Drawing XIII,* it is a composition of lines, shapes, and tones but now with a new element: color.

Sometimes Georgia made her work just *seem* abstract by painting a subject from an unusual perspective, such as very close up or very far away, or by showing only part of it. The six paintings in the jack-in-the-pulpit series are an example of this. The first picture is of the whole flower; the last is a close-up of the jack, the central rod inside the flower. Without looking at the title of the last painting or seeing it with the others in the series, we probably would not be able to guess that it is of a flower.

Georgia also did a number of paintings inspired by views out of airplane windows. When she painted rivers after seeing them from so high above, they became twisting lines. Georgia always saw things in new ways.

Georgia and Alfred Stieglitz continued to live in New York City but summered in upstate New York at Lake George. While Georgia did many paintings of New York City skyscrapers, she was happier working in the country surrounded by weathered barns, larkspur, and hollyhocks.

Black Hollyhock, Blue Larkspur shows Georgia's love of flowers and how taken she was with their shapes and colors. For Georgia they seemed to be the essence of life. In fact, flowers were one of her favorite subjects. She painted them large because she wanted people to see in them what she saw. "I'll paint what I see—what the flower is to me, but I'll paint it big and they will be surprised into taking time to look at it—I will make even busy New Yorkers take time to see what I see of flowers."

In 1929, Georgia visited New Mexico with a friend and now fell in love all over again, but this time with the desert. Although she continued to live with Stieglitz for part of every year, she spent many months alone in the Southwest, painting the land and objects she found there—the stones and the feathers

Black Hollyhock, Blue Larkspur, 1929.

From the Faraway Nearby, 1937.

and bones left by decayed animals. The desert had a special power for Georgia. The land seemed to go on forever and touched that mysterious feeling about nature she had always had.

From the Faraway Nearby shows both the clarity of the desert air and the spaciousness of the landscape. It is a mysterious painting. A large pair of elk antlers floats in the air very close to the viewer, while in the far distance are snow-capped mountains. Nothing is in the middle.

In 1946, a few years after Stieglitz died, Georgia moved permanently to New Mexico. While she continued to paint with absolute dedication, she also loved to walk around the land with her two chow dogs, taking in the mountain views, the sunrises and sunsets, the lines of cattle grazing along the horizon. Georgia painted till she was almost blind and lived in the desert until her death, in 1986, at the age of ninety-eight.

Georgia O'Keeffe's paintings have given us a unique vision of America. In them we see a land that is vast and pure, clear and unexplainable, all at the same time. They are about America, but they are also about Georgia Totto O'Keeffe.

Frida Kahlo

Frida Kahlo in 1931, when she was twenty-four years old.

Frida Kahlo was born on July 6, 1907, in a bright blue house in Coyoacán, Mexico, just outside Mexico City.

She was a round little girl with a dimple in her chin and a mischievous smile. Early on, her mother, Matilde, taught her to cook, sew, embroider, and clean—all the things Mexican girls were supposed to know. She also tried to instill religion in her four daughters, but Frida and her younger sister, Christina, sometimes rebelled. When the other family members would pray before meals, Frida and Christina would secretly glance at each other, trying not to laugh. Sometimes they would escape from their catechism class to eat the fruit in a nearby orchard.

Frida's father, Guillermo, was a professional photographer and an amateur painter and philosopher. He loved Frida very much and took great pleasure in teaching her about the many things that interested him. Nature was his passion. Rocks, birds, flowers, animals, shells, and insects all became an exciting part of Frida's life. Sometimes Guillermo and Frida would go to a neighborhood park; while he painted, she would find insects and plants to dissect and study. When Frida was older, Guillermo taught her about Mexican archeology and art and about photography as well.

When Frida was six years of age, though, her life changed dramatically. She was stricken with polio and was confined to her room for nine months. The disease was painful and left her right leg shorter and thinner than her left one.

Frida became more quiet as a result of her illness. She created an imaginary friend, a girl her own age to whom she could talk during her long hours in bed. This friend helped her feel less lonely and later even became a character in a painting, *The Two Fridas,* in which two women who look just like Frida hold hands. The idea that her imagination could comfort her stayed with her all her life.

As Frida recovered, her father encouraged her to swim, skate, wrestle, box, bicycle, and play ball to strengthen her leg. She did all of these and did them well, but she was teased by her playmates anyway. They called her *"Frida, pata de palo"* ("Frida, peg leg"). Frida became more outgoing as she grew up, getting a reputation as a "character." Still, she sometimes felt left out and alone.

When Frida was fifteen, she went to the best preparatory school in Mexico. She was very bright and planned to become a doctor when she grew up. She and her group of friends, mostly boys, were known for their pranks and occasionally got into trouble. Once some of them rode a donkey through the halls of the school.

When Frida was eighteen, another tragedy happened, and her life was changed forever. One day

Frida at age five.

a trolley car hit her school bus and she was flung into the street. Her spine, collarbone, ribs, pelvis, and right leg (the one that had been weakened by polio) were broken. Her right foot was dislocated and crushed. Worst of all, a steel handrail pierced her stomach. The doctors were not sure she would survive.

Frida was determined to live, though, and she did. Then, the summer after the accident, she had the

Frida's needlepoint *The Little House,* done when she was eight years old.

first of many relapses. Once again she had to be bedridden. While during her recovery from polio she was required to be active, now she was forced to be still. She had to wear a brace and could not even sit up.

It was at this time that she began to paint. Her father lent her a box of oil paints, and her mother had a special easel built so that Frida could paint while lying in bed.

Her first paintings were mostly portraits of the people around her—her friends and her family. In several of them she copied the style of famous European painters. Only one hinted that she would develop into an unusual artist. It was a self-portrait, sad and delicate but also strong.

When Frida was well enough, she took her paintings to show a famous Mexican artist, Diego Rivera. Diego was a huge, funny-looking man who painted enormous murals throughout Mexico. He told Frida that he thought she had talent, and he particularly admired the originality of her self-portrait. Frida and Diego started seeing each other and soon fell in love. Eventually they were married.

Frida began painting more seriously after she met Diego. His encouragement must have meant a great deal to her, and she found his ideas exciting. Diego's paintings, often on the walls of public buildings, told

Frieda and Diego Rivera, 1931.
Frida's given name was *Frieda.* She eventually dropped the *e.*

stories of Mexican peasants and their struggles to survive. He and his friends believed that the native art of Mexico, the art of the Mexican people, was the best art. Before, many people in the art world had looked down on Mexican art, and Mexican artists had tried to paint like Europeans. Frida was influenced by these ideas and began to paint pictures that were more Mexican in feeling. She even began to dress up in Mexican clothes and decorate her home with Mexican art.

Frieda and Diego Rivera shows Diego's influence on Frida. She depicted him as a great artist, gripping his brushes and palette in one hand and lightly holding her hand in the other. She showed herself as his admiring wife, dressed up in a Mexican costume, her body turned slightly toward him. The blue-green, pink, lavender, orange, and brown colors she used are common in Mexican art. The message on the ribbon above her head gives the date and occasion for the painting. Diego, too, sometimes included ribbons with messages in his work; this device was used in many old Mexican paintings.

While Frida was influenced by Diego's ideas, her work was very different from his. Her paintings were small and personal, not huge and public. She often used herself as her model, creating different scenes with Mexican plants and animals, usually her pets.

Fulang-Chang and I, or *Self-Portrait,* 1937.

Fulang-Chang and I is one of the most playful of Frida's self-portraits. In it she painted herself with a pet monkey and emphasized the similarity of their features. Frida had many pets—dogs, cats, birds, and a deer as well as monkeys. She liked to think of herself as an animal, too.

In *My Grandparents, My Parents, and I* Frida painted her family tree. She showed herself at about age two standing in the patio of her Coyoacán house. She is holding a blood-red ribbon that joins her with her parents and grandparents, who float like clouds in the sky, the way people were often shown in old photographs. Her mother's parents, of Mexican-Indian and Spanish descent, appear above the Mexican land, while her father's parents, who were Europeans, appear above the ocean. Frida herself stands naked, with her bare feet planted on the Mexican ground. She has connected herself with her past, with the earth, and with Mexico.

Frida's love of detail also comes through in this painting. She copied every ruffle and bow in her mother's wedding dress. In the skirt is an accurately drawn developing fetus, perhaps Frida before she was born.

As Frida grew as an artist, her paintings showed more of her feelings. Because she was often sad, many of her paintings illustrate the sad part of her life.

My Grandparents, My Parents, and I (Family Tree), 1936.

Memory, 1937.

Frida never recovered from her accident and had many operations to try to straighten her spine and repair her foot. She was often in pain. In addition, while she loved Diego and he loved her, he did not always treat her very well, and she was unhappy much of the time. They did get divorced for a short while but remarried because they loved and needed each other. Frida, also, was unable to have children and that, perhaps, made her the saddest of all. Her painting became a way for her to express her inner experience. Even if that experience was horrifying, she painted it.

Frida's painting *Memory* speaks of her loneliness and the sorrow she felt in love as well as of her physical suffering. She showed herself as helpless and wounded. She has no arms, and her heart is on the ground. Her body is pierced by a rod with a small cupid on each end, as if sitting on a seesaw. Tears streak down her cheeks toward the ocean at her feet. Her bandaged foot resembles a small sailboat that is stranded on a beach. She is standing all alone between her childhood clothes and a Mexican costume that she often wore with Diego.

In *The Little Deer,* Frida is again injured. Here she is a deer running through the forest but struck by many arrows. The trees are dried and cracked as though they are dying. A branch from a young tree is broken and lying at her feet.

The Little Deer, 1946.

Not all Frida's work is so sad. In *Roots* she is lying on the Pedregal, a vast region of volcanic rock in Mexico. Little can grow there, and yet from a hole in Frida's body springs forth a luxuriant green vine. It appears that Frida's body is part of the land. Her life cycle and the cycle of nature are one.

In Frida's everyday life, she tried to be happy. She often dressed up in bright costumes with long skirts and wore lots of jewelry. She would also arrange her hair in the styles of different regions of Mexico, decorating it with ribbons, bows, clips, combs, or fresh flowers. She liked to go to parties and to spend time relaxing with her friends. She also worked with her friends to change the Mexican government.

Roots, 1943.

Frida's artwork started to become known, even outside of Mexico. André Breton, a French poet and founder of an artists' group called the Surrealists, organized a showing of her paintings in Paris. He thought Frida's work was so powerful that he called it "a ribbon around a bomb."

Unfortunately, Frida's health declined. In her forties she became weaker and weaker. A Mexican gallery wanted to have a major exhibition of Frida's art at this time, and Frida said yes. With her lively spirit and flair for the dramatic, she arranged to have her four-poster bed carried into the gallery. She decorated it with papier-mâché skeletons and photographs of Diego and her political heroes. When the show opened, she was placed on the bed wearing a beautiful Mexican gown. Over two hundred people came to greet her, and all gathered around and sang Mexican songs.

On July 13, 1954, a little over a year after that wonderful celebration, Frida died in the bright blue house in Coyoacán, in the room where she was born.

Now we have Frida's art to remember her by. It shows us a brave and talented woman who used her art to fight many of life's obstacles. It is frightening work sometimes, but it is also a reminder of the strength a woman can have.

Self-Portrait, painted about the year 1938.

Alice Neel

Alice Neel with her granddaughter Olivia in 1974.
The painting in the upper left is of Olivia.

Alice Neel was born on January 28, 1900. She grew up in Colwyn, Pennsylvania, a small town near Philadelphia. Although Alice's neighborhood had once been a pear orchard and was still quite beautiful, she despised it. She felt there was nothing to do in Colwyn and was bored.

Her mother, Alice Concross Hartley, was a strong-willed woman who could trace her ancestors to one of the signers of the Declaration of Independence. While she was intelligent and well read, she was also unhappy and difficult. When Alice was a child and thinking about what to do with her life, her mother said, "I don't know what you expect to do in the world; you're only a girl."

Her father, George Washington Neel, was a clerk for the Pennsylvania Railroad. He was kind, supportive, and philosophical.

As a child, Alice was extremely sensitive. Many things frightened her, even common things like a toy stuffed cat. People's feelings affected her greatly, too. Sometimes she would try to please others so much that she would stop being herself.

Like Georgia O'Keeffe, Alice wasn't sure how she got the idea, but she always knew she wanted to be an artist. She remembered being eight years old and thinking her watercolors and painting book were her most important possessions. She liked to paint flowers, fruit, and romantic couples. During high school, she didn't study art but used to draw heads in the margins of her school papers.

Alice also excelled in math and became a skilled stenographer and typist. Because she didn't want to burden her family financially, after graduation she worked at a secretarial job. Without telling anyone, she went to art school at night.

At one school she attended, her teacher had definite ideas about how one should paint. When Alice tried to paint hair the way she thought best, the teacher became annoyed. He yelled, "Before you can conquer art, you'll have to conquer yourself. Even if you paint for forty years you may not get anywhere." Alice paid no attention. "That's not for you to say because you are only my *beginning* teacher," she replied.

Later she enrolled in the Philadelphia School of Design for Women. She saved enough money to pay for one year of classes and then, because she was talented, received scholarships. She chose this school because she knew she would have the freedom to

Alice Neel in 1905, at age five.

paint as she liked there. At the well-known Pennsylvania Academy of the Fine Arts, the students were taught to paint like the Impressionists, the French school of artists who painted bright, sunny landscapes. Alice never felt comfortable painting happy subjects. She always felt close to those who suffer. Even if she was painting flowers, she would portray them with such intense colors and lines that the pictures would seem to be about life and death, not just about beauty.

Although Alice had a lot of freedom at the school she chose, her work was still sometimes too rough for her teachers. Once she painted a brick wall that was chipped and partially covered with ivy. She later said that her teachers would have preferred a "neat, tidy wall done with a ruler."

Alice worked so hard in art school that she became completely exhausted. To help her regain her strength, her parents sent her to an art school in the country outside of Philadelphia during the summer of 1924. There she met Carlos Enriquez, another art student, who soon became her husband.

Carlos was from a very wealthy family in Cuba. They owned a lot of land and even had servants. In 1926, Alice went to live with Carlos and his family in Havana, Cuba. There she had her first exhibition.

Instead of painting the lush foliage of this tropical

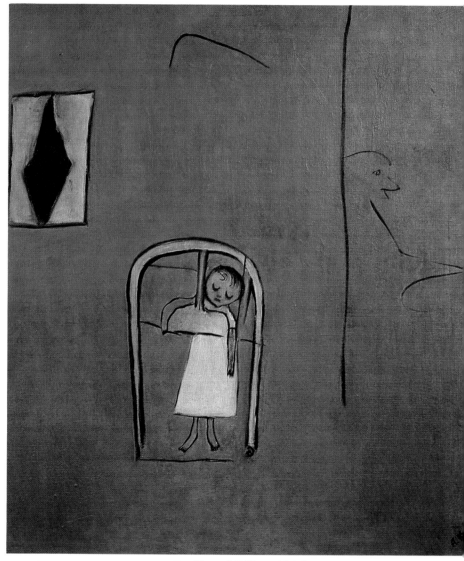

Futility of Effort, 1930.

island or the well-to-do people, Alice painted the poor and the old. She also did a few cheerful paintings, though. They were of her daughter, Santillana, who was born in Cuba.

In 1927, Alice and Carlos returned to New York City with Santillana to try to live as artists. Then something terrible happened. Santillana became ill and, in the winter, died of diphtheria.

Alice was filled with grief and painted *Futility of Effort* to express her feelings. It is a simple, almost childlike black, white, and gray painting, with few lines. It shows a little girl, eyes closed, hanging limply from the edge of her bed. One can feel Alice's sadness and hopelessness at the loss of her daughter.

Alice became pregnant again right away. In 1928 she had another daughter, Isabetta. They continued to stay in New York City, struggling to live with help from their families. After two and a half difficult years, however, Carlos returned to Havana with Isabetta, leaving Alice alone.

Carlos' trip to Cuba was to be just a visit. His parents had promised to send Alice and him to Paris, but when he arrived in Havana they refused. The Great Depression, which was triggered by the stock market crash of 1929, had caused their sugar business to suffer, and they no longer wanted to give him the money. Carlos ended up traveling to Paris,

anyway, with the help of his friends, but he went there without Alice.

At first, with more time to paint, Alice worked furiously. She painted people mostly, friends and neighbors, but also some landscapes and still lifes. Then she received a letter from Carlos and realized that Isabetta and he were not going to return. She was not to see her daughter again for three years. Alice became so depressed that she needed to be hospitalized.

At the hospital the doctors didn't believe she was a professional artist. They wouldn't let her draw or paint. Of course, that made her feel worse. Luckily, after a few months, a social worker visited her and brought her pencils and paper. Alice began to draw the other patients and was so good at it that one doctor wanted her to draw him. She refused, but she continued to draw. Working helped her get well. Alice once said that the only time she found peace was when she painted. "The minute I sat in front of a canvas," she said, "I was happy. Because it was a world, and I could do as I liked in it."

Alice's luck did not change, however. After her recovery, she lived with a sailor who tended to be very jealous. One day, in a fit of anger, he destroyed much of her work—over two hundred and fifty pictures. Alice was again stricken with grief. She felt

Synthesis of New York: The Great Depression, 1933.

compelled to move to a new neighborhood where she could begin again.

By now, some people in the New York City art world knew Alice as an artist. In 1933, she was asked to work for the Public Works of Art Project. Two years later, she joined the Federal Art Project of the Works Progress Administration, or the WPA. Both of these programs were started by the United States government to help artists during the Depression. Alice would have to give the government one painting every six weeks. In return she would receive about thirty dollars a week, a good salary in those days. She accepted. This was the first time Alice got paid for her work and the first time she had enough money for food, rent, and art supplies.

Much of Alice's work shows us about the times in which she lived. This is especially true of the paintings she did during the Depression. *Synthesis of New York (The Great Depression)* is one of several powerful New York street scenes she created during the 1930s. It shows people with skull heads in a dreary New York setting. It is as if the life has been beaten out of them by the hard times. Once Alice said, "If I could, I would make the world happy; the wretched faces in the subway, sad and full of troubles, worry me."

Alice joined a political group, the Communist

Party. While she was too shy to speak up at meetings, she liked to paint the members and their demonstrations. *Nazis Murder Jews* is one such painting. It is of a torchlight parade staged by the Communists to protest the killing of the Jews in Germany. In the foreground, people carry a sign that says: "Nazis Murder Jews." Alice painted the sign large because she believed that art can deeply affect people's lives. She later said that if more people had seen her painting and read that sign, more Jews could have been saved.

In 1938, Alice settled in Spanish Harlem, an area in New York City where many Latin people live. Alice felt at home in this neighborhood and lived there for the next twenty years. She always had a large apartment so she would have space to paint. She used to ask anyone who was visually interesting to pose for a painting. Often she painted her neighbors' children.

Two Black Girls, also called *Antonia and Carmen Encarnaçion,* shows two little Puerto Rican girls who lived upstairs from Alice. Their expressions, the angle of their heads, and the way one is holding her face portray a sadness and a longing. Their lives must have been difficult, for they seem to be saying, "Can you help us?"

Alice was always very sensitive to other people.

Two Black Girls, or *Antonia and Carmen Encarnaçion,* 1959.

Richard at Age Five, 1944.

While being that way was sometimes difficult, it was an advantage for her as an artist. Her paintings of people are not like photographs. She seemed to see inside a person, to see a person's feelings. That's what makes Alice's art so special.

By 1941, Alice had two sons, Richard and Hartley. She also had her first New York City exhibition. Painting her family, her children, and later, her daughters-in-law and her grandchildren became more and more important to her. She painted all of them at different stages of their lives.

Richard at Age 5 is a portrait of her older son. He is seated on a chair but seems to be right in front of us. The warm colors of the paints contrast with the seriousness of his expression. His eyes are so wide and penetrating that he seems to be looking at us more intensely than we are looking at him.

Hartley on the Rocking Horse shows Alice's younger son. He, too, seems to be popping off the canvas. This blonde-haired child is filled with emotion, expressing the wild energy of a growing toddler. Looking carefully to the left of Hartley, we can see Alice in the mirror, painting.

Subconscious is a different kind of portrait. It is like a dream, telling us about Alice's inner feelings. It was painted on winter nights in Harlem when Alice was alone with two young children. Alice is in the center holding her son Richard. Around the edges of the picture, she painted "the gods of sickness," make-believe spirits to keep away illness.

While Alice was happy to exhibit her paintings, they did not sell. She still had trouble making enough money to survive. The government program that helped her ended in 1943. Alice became quite discouraged, but she did not change the way she painted.

Perhaps people did not like her style because it is not pretty. She shows emotions that many people have trouble accepting in themselves. Often her sitters appear vulnerable, anxious, fearful, or filled with pain. In this regard, Alice's portraits are very different from most other portraits. Generally people have paid artists to paint their pictures; as a result, portrait painters have tended to flatter their subjects. Alice did not expect her subjects to buy her work. She valued showing the truth above all else.

The way in which Alice applied paint also was not popular. She would work quickly, trying to capture the most outstanding features and feelings of her subjects as well as her own spontaneous reactions. In doing this, she used rough brushstrokes and sometimes left areas of the canvas without any paint at all. "I hate pictures that make you think of all the work that was done to create them," she said.

While Alice continued to exhibit from time to time, it was not until 1962 that her art began to be more accepted. That year, a well-known art historian picked one of her paintings to be bought and then given to a university in New Orleans, Louisiana. Also, a major New York art magazine *Art News* published an article about her work.

A wealthy woman who had seen Alice's paintings and loved them came to her studio to buy several.

Alice Neel in her Harlem studio in 1948, when she was forty-eight years old.

Subconscious, 1942.

When she saw the impoverished circumstances under which Alice lived, she offered to help her. She gave Alice an allowance so that she could just paint and not worry about anything else.

At the same time, Alice visited a psychologist who encouraged her to show her work to more gallery owners. Alice was always shy and sometimes had trouble asking people to sit for her. Talking to the psychologist helped. She began to show her work to more people and now, to her surprise, they loved it. She started to have more exhibitions and began to paint many new people—all kinds of people, including famous artists, politicians, and an archbishop.

All the while, she continued to paint her friends and her family. Mothers and children remained one of her favorite themes. *Mother and Child (Nancy and Olivia)* is of her son Richard's wife, Nancy, and their oldest child. Unlike most mother and child paintings that show the happiness of motherhood, this one clearly expresses the nervousness a new mother feels trying to take care of her energetic baby. Olivia looks as though she is squirming. Nancy is trying to hold on to her. The background, which is distorted, emphasizes their movement. It is as if the entire canvas is shaking with anxiety.

Hartley on the Rocking Horse, 1943.

Mother and Child (Nancy and Olivia), 1967.

Soon Alice was asked to join a New York City gallery. She began to receive awards, too, like the American Academy and Institute of Arts and Letters' Arts and Letters Award, given to her by the President of the United States.

In 1974, the Whitney Museum of American Art gave a major showing of fifty-eight of her paintings! The next year, the Georgia Museum of Art held an even larger exhibition and published a thick catalogue as well.

Alice died in New York City in 1984, but her life ended with much satisfaction. She stuck to her ideals, never changing her art to please others in spite of many hardships. She once said with humor, "All experience is great providing you live through it." We are fortunate that Alice was so courageous. With her strength, she was able to pursue her vision and give the world many treasures.

Faith Ringgold

Faith Ringgold in 1987.

When Faith Ringgold was born in Harlem Hospital in 1930, her mother, Willi Posey Jones, was sad. She had lost her eighteen-month-old son to pneumonia just six months before. A nurse suggested to Willi that she name her new daughter Faith. Willi liked the name and agreed it was a time to have faith.

The 1930s were the years of the Great Depression, when most people in America were struggling to make a living. Luckily, Faith's father, Andrew Jones, had a good job driving a truck for the New York City Sanitation Department. His income provided security for the family, which included two older children, Andrew Jr. and Barbara, as well as Faith.

Faith was a sickly child. She had asthma so badly that often she had to stay home from school. Faith's mother took excellent care of her. Willi not only helped Faith feel better physically but also taught her lessons so that she would not fall behind.

Even more important, without realizing it, Faith's mother helped her to become an artist. When Faith was recovering in bed and had finished her studies, her mother would bring her crayons and paper, needles, thread, and fabric, all to create whatever she liked. Because Faith's mother was a fashion designer and dressmaker, she showed Faith many ways of working with cloth. Faith enjoyed these times with her mother a lot.

Faith's mother also did other special things for her. Because Faith was allergic to many foods, Willi made her special cookies and drinks to take to school for snacks. She sewed her special clothes, too, like her green gym suit. All the children wore green gym suits, but Faith's was of a different style.

Faith Ringgold in 1931, when she was one year old.

When Faith felt better, her mother took her on outings to museums. They also went downtown to see the "Stars," famous musicians like Benny Goodman, Duke Ellington, and Judy Garland. To Faith, each of these performers was *somebody*. She knew her mother wanted her to be somebody, and now she could understand what that meant. She, too, would be a Star, she thought. Someday.

Faith learned from her father, too. Although her parents divorced when she was young, her father spent his days off with her. He helped teach her to read and bought her first drawing board and easel.

All these experiences made Faith feel different from other children but special. Though she was sometimes lonely, her sense of being different was an important part of her becoming an artist, for an artist makes artwork unlike anybody else's. Another thing helped, too. To be an artist, one needs self-confidence. Faith gained that confidence from the love and encouragement her mother and father provided.

When Faith graduated from high school in 1948, she knew she wanted to be an artist. She tried to enroll at the City College of New York in liberal arts, but at that time, the school would not allow women to be liberal arts students. Women *were* allowed to enroll as education students, however. Because Faith's mother wanted her to be a teacher as her grandparents had been, Faith decided that she would enroll in the School of Education. Then she would teach art for a living and do her own creative work in her spare hours.

In 1955, Faith began a career as a teacher in the New York City public schools. She taught children from kindergarten through college for almost twenty years. It was hard but rewarding work. Faith learned many things from her students. Whenever she wanted to use a new material, she would first give it to them. She found the youngest ones the most original and fresh in their approach. They often helped her see new ways of doing things.

In one class, a student brought in an article written about her brother, James Baldwin, a powerful black writer. Faith started reading his work as well as the work of other black writers such as Amiri Baraka, then called LeRoi Jones. These authors gave Faith a sense of pride in being black. Their words triggered new ideas that she wanted to put into her paintings. Until now, she had painted mostly landscapes that expressed her feelings about nature.

Her new work began to speak of the struggles of black Americans. She knew blacks did not have as many opportunities as whites and were sometimes mistreated. Her painting *U.S. Postage Stamp*

Commemorating the Advent of Black Power is a response to the unfair advantage that white people have. It exhibits one hundred faces; ninety are white, and ten are black. The words *white power* are spelled out in large white letters dividing the faces. *Black power* is also spelled out, in smaller black letters placed diagonally across the canvas. The entire painting is like a large postage stamp. It expresses Faith's desire to send a message: inequality is wrong and must be stopped.

She called her early political paintings her *American People Series*. She had to struggle to have the art world recognize them, but eventually she was able to show them in galleries and special exhibitions. One such exhibition represented the first time black artists had displayed their work in Harlem, New York City's largest black community, in thirty years!

She also began to try to create more opportunities for blacks and women. By demonstrating with others, she got museums to show the work of black women artists and to put more blacks in decision-making positions.

Although Faith was discouraged at times because she had to fight for these changes, she continued to be optimistic. "I never wanted to look back and be bitter," she said. "I don't feel strong. I just feel like the train is coming into the station and if I don't get

Aunt Bessie and *Aunt Edith,* 1974.

on it, it's going to be gone and I won't be on it. You can't catch it later."

The biggest change in Faith's art life came in 1972, while she was teaching an African arts class at Bank Street College. A student who had just seen Faith's exhibition of watercolor paintings questioned her. She didn't understand why Faith, who loved to teach her students how to work with beads and fabric, never used these materials in her own art.

Faith didn't like being questioned, but she knew her student was right. She realized she was ignoring not only her childhood experiences but also her interest in African culture and her heritage as a woman and a black American. In Faith's family, women had worked with cloth for generations. Faith had learned such skills from her mother, and Faith's mother had learned from Faith's great-grandmother Betsy Bingham. Willi had watched Betsy boil and bleach flour sacks till they were pure white in order to line her quilts. Faith's great-great-grandmother Susie Shannon also sewed quilts. She had been a slave and made them as part of her duties as "house girl" for a plantation owner.

That summer Faith visited an art museum in Europe and for the first time saw tankas, Tibetan paintings mounted on cloth. Seeing this cloth art made her realize she could work in this way, too.

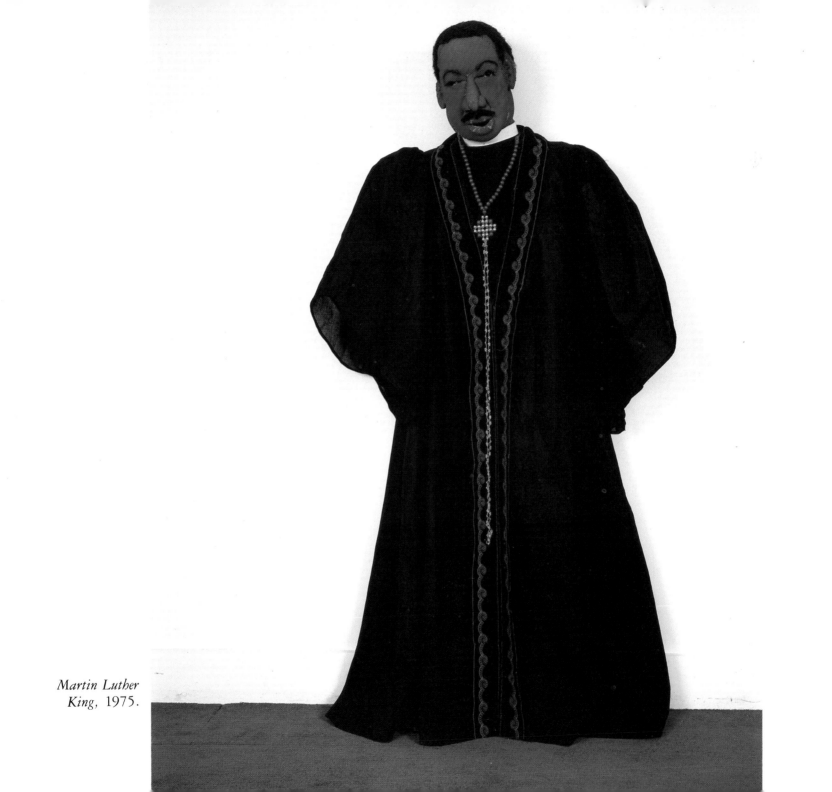

*Martin Luther
King,* 1975.

Now Faith's work really blossomed. She found that with cloth she could combine all her interests—her political ideas, her fondness for African art, and her experiences growing up as a black female in New York City's Harlem. She left her teaching position so that she could work on her art full-time. She began sewing her own tankas and masks, sometimes with the help of her mother.

Edith and *Bessie* are two life-size cloth masks from this period. They are portraits of Faith's aunts, but they are not portraits in the ordinary American sense. Like African masks, they are meant to show the kind of people the aunts were, not how they actually looked. Because Aunt Edith was blind and depended on Bessie, these two masks are often shown together. They can be worn, much the way a costume is worn, but can also be hung from the ceiling or wall. Faith used many materials to make them. The heads are painted canvas, and the dresses are beaded, fringed, and embroidered cloth. The mouths of the aunts are open to show the need for women to speak out. One of the aunts wears a whistle to get attention.

Martin Luther King is another mask that can be worn. It is larger than life-size, showing the importance of the slain civil rights leader. King's head, made from foam rubber, is sewn and painted in such a way as to make the face look just like him.

Lena, 1978.

Sonny's Quilt, 1986.

Faith even let the stitching show to represent his wounds.

As Faith's soft art developed, she began to make sculpture and, eventually, quilts. *Lena* is a soft sculpture of a homeless woman in Harlem. She is only seventeen inches tall but seems very real. Her face, which is made from a stuffed stocking, is nipped and pulled to look like the face of a woman who lives on the street. While it is painful to see the sculpture of a homeless person, Faith believes it is important not to forget there are suffering people living in America.

Faith also began to use her soft art to tell stories. She learned the art of storytelling from her mother, who was an expert. The entire family—relatives who lived nearby as well as close neighbors —would come to hear Willi tell tales of past experiences and future dreams. Faith remembers being fascinated as she would sit and listen to her mother's entertaining adventures.

Faith's art sometimes tells stories with pictures but no words, as in *Sonny's Quilt*. Sonny is Sonny Rollins, the well-known jazz musician with whom Faith grew up. She created this quilt to celebrate his dedication as an artist. Faith remembers him always looking for an out-of-the-way place to practice his horn so that he wouldn't disturb anyone. He used his closet, but

The Women: Mask Face Quilt I, 1986.

Dinner Quilt, 1986.

his favorite place was a walkway on a bridge in New York City.

Like most of her work, *The Women: Mask Face Quilt 1* shows us Faith's love of Harlem. Each face is based on someone she knew or saw there. Together they represent a wide variety of human types. The bright colors and bold patterns celebrate the liveliness of this community where she has lived since she was a little girl.

In other work, Faith tells stories with pictures *and* words. In *The Dinner Quilt*, the words are those of a woman named Melody remembering past Christmas dinners with her family at her Aunt Connie's. As children, she and Connie's son, Lonnie, would play doctor under the piano and listen in on the mysterious conversations of the adults. Aunt Connie was especially memorable: she embroidered names of famous black women on place mats and assigned seats to all the family members. "Melody," she would say, "you sit with Sojourner Truth and your ma and pa next to you with Fannie Lou Hamer and Marian Anderson." Now Christmas dinner is different for Melody. She has grown up and become a lawyer. She is planning to invite Lonnie, a handsome businessman, over for an elegant meal.

With her talent for storytelling, Faith also developed performances to be acted out with her work. These productions, which she has been asked to do throughout the United States, often involve singing, dancing, chanting, and audience participation.

One such artwork and performance is *Change: Faith Ringgold's Over 100 Pounds Weight Loss Story Quilt.* Created in 1985 and 1986, it describes Faith's loss of more than one hundred pounds and records her own history of eating. In between the text, the fabric is printed with photographs of Faith from her early childhood to the present. The colorful borders are tie-dyed, bringing to mind the warm, rich patterns of African cloth.

This quilt is the centerpiece for a performance Faith gives. Draped in a jacket made from a copy of the quilt, she appears in front of an audience, dragging a black plastic bag filled with water. She soon leaves the bag because it is so heavy, but from time to time returns to try, unsuccessfully, to move it again. All the while she recites the text of the quilt. She ends by taking off the jacket and chanting, "I can do it. I can change, I can change. Now!" She invites the audience to join her in chanting and dancing to the song "Only the Strong Survive." The quilt and the performance are Faith's message to the world that with work, good things are possible.

In the 1980s, Faith's art began to get more

1930-1939 →

In the 1930's folks had fried chicken and greens for Sunday dinner, and fried fish and potato salad on Friday. Your family had leg of mutton on Sunday and fried fish on Saturday. Fried fish was the only food your mother fried when you were a kid 'cause nobody ever heard of porgies cooked any other way. Because

You had asthma and were allergic, you were on a health food diet of steamed vegetables, fresh fruit, lamb, chicken, veal, skimmed milk, corn meal gruel, and homemade lemon ice cream made with skimmed milk that tasted awful.

Your mother never allowed you to eat between meals. The kitchen was closed every evening after supper till breakfast the next morning. Years later you developed a fascination for late night eating by the light of the open refrigerator door. You thought those calories didn't count. But what about the tell-tale evidence they left behind and in front?

Exercise was part of the days work for your mother. You were up before dawn in the morning; bathed, dressed, and out in the street; then back for lunch and a nap; out again, back for dinner and in bed before sundown. Vacations were spent on the beach in Atlantic City. But mothers schedule was unchanged. While you were napping you could hear her snapping her fingers and dancing to William B. Williams radio program: "It's Make Believe Ballroom Time" while she did her housework. That was her aerobic exercise, and it took you all these years to figure that out.

(1) Faith 1931; (2) with Barbara 1937; (3) with Barbara at World Fair 1939; (4) with Barbara and Andrew 1938; (5) with Barbara and Andrew 1931; (6) on beach in Atlantic City 1938; (7) with Mother 1936; (8) in buggy 1931; (9) with Andrew and Barbara at 3yr old birthday, 1938; (10) with Andrew on boardwalk in Atlantic City 1936; (11) with Barbara and Andrew 1937; (12) with Mother and Barbara (in sand) in Atlantic City 1936; (13) with Andrew and Barbara 1936; (14) Faith 1937; (15) with Barbara and Andrew, Orange N.J. 1931; (16) with Andrew and Barbara in snow 1933; (17) with Barbara on beach in Atlantic City 1938

Photo Credits: DeLaigle Studios

Part of *Change: Faith Ringgold's Over 100 Pounds Weight Loss Story Quilt*, 1986-1987.

attention. In 1984, she was asked to have a major showing of her work over the past twenty years. The exhibit was to be in the same building in which she had her first exhibition, now called the Studio Museum in Harlem. The exhibit was such a success that many newspapers wrote about it, including the *New York Times*. A year later, Faith was also asked to be a full professor at the University of California in San Diego. She accepted and now lives half of the year in California and the other half in New York.

As a woman and a black American, Faith has sometimes encountered opposition to her work. Yet with the love of her family and the community support of Harlem, she has been able to achieve her goals. She has said, "I don't believe in not seeing the negative. But you can take that negative and make it positive. Change the form and you can change your life."

Faith Ringgold and her art continue to grow and change.

Picture Credits

Georgia O'Keeffe

6   Georgia O'Keeffe, July 19, 1915. Holsinger Studio Collection, University of Virginia Library.

7   *Blue and Green Music* (1919).
Oil on canvas, 23″ x 19″, 1969.835.
© 1987 The Art Institute of Chicago. All Rights Reserved.

8   *Jack-in-the-Pulpit I* (1943).
Oil on canvas, 12″ x 9″.
Courtesy of ACA Gallery, New York.

10   Drawing XIII (1915).
Charcoal on paper, 24½″ x 19″.
©1950 By The Metropolitan Museum of Art, The Alfred Stieglitz Collection. (50.236.2) Photograph by Malcolm Varon.

12   *Evening Star III* (1917).
Watercolor, 9″ x 11⅞″.
Collection, The Museum of Modern Art, New York.
Mr. and Mrs. Donald Strauss Fund.

13   *Light Coming on the Plains II* (1917).
Watercolor on paper, 11⅞″ x 8⅞″.
Amon Carter Museum, Fort Worth.

15   *Black Hollyhock, Blue Larkspur* (1929).
Oil on canvas, 36″ x 30″.
©1934 By The Metropolitan Museum of Art, George A. Hearn Fund. (34.51) Photograph by Lynton Gardiner.

16   *From the Faraway Nearby* (1937).
Oil on canvas, 36″ x 40⅛″.
©1959 By The Metropolitan Museum of Art, The Alfred Stieglitz Collection. (59.204.2)

Frida Kahlo

18   Frida Kahlo, 1931.
Photograph by Imogen Cunningham.
© The Imogen Cunningham Trust.

19   Frida at age five.
Photo: Guillermo Kahlo.

20   *The Little House* (1915).
Needlepoint. 11 cm. x 18½ cm.
Collection: Isolda Pinedo Kahlo.
Photo: Dr. Solomón Grimberg.

21   *Frieda and Diego Rivera* (1931).
Oil on canvas, 39⅜″ x 31″.
San Francisco Museum of Modern Art,
Albert M. Bender Collection, gift of Albert M. Bender.

22   *Self-Portrait* (1937).
Oil on masonite. 25¼″ x 19″ x 2½″.
Collection, The Museum of Modern Art,
New York. Mary Sklar Bequest.

23   *My Grandparents, My Parents, and I (Family Tree)* (1936).
Oil and tempera on metal panel, 12⅛″ x 13⅝″.
Collection, The Museum of Modern Art, New York. Gift of Allan Ross, M.D., and B. Mathieu Roos.

24   *Memory* (1937).
Oil on tin, 15¾″ x 11″.
Private Collection. Photo: Dr. Solomón Grimberg.

25   *The Little Deer* (1946).
Oil on canvas. 9″ x 12″.
Private Collection. Photo: Sotheby Parke Bernet.

26   *Roots* (1943).
Oil on sheet metal, 11¾″ x 14½″. Private Collection.

27   *Self-Portrait* (c. 1938).
Oil on aluminum and glass, 11½″ x 8½″.
Musée National d'Art Moderne, Centre Georges Pompidou, Paris.

Alice Neel

All work courtesy Robert Miller Gallery, New York.

2,37 *Hartley on the Rocking Horse* (1943).
Oil on canvas, 30" x 34".

28 Alice Neel with her granddaughter Olivia, 1974.

29 Alice Neel in 1905, at age five.

30 *Futility of Effort* (1930).
Oil on canvas, 26¼" x 24½". Private Collection.

32 *Synthesis of New York: The Great Depression* (1933).
Oil on canvas, 48" x 39".

33 *Two Black Girls,* or *Antonia and Carmen Encarnaçion* (1959).
Oil on canvas, 30" x 25".

34 *Richard at Age Five* (1944).
Oil on canvas, 26" x 14".

35 Alice Neel in her Harlem studio, 1948.

36 *Subconscious* (1942).
Oil on canvas, 28" x 24".

38 *Mother and Child (Nancy and Olivia)* (1967).
Oil on canvas, 42" x 34". Private Collection.

Faith Ringgold

All work courtesy Bernice Steinbaum Gallery, New York.

40 Faith Ringgold, 1987.
Photo: C. Love.

41 Faith Ringgold in 1931, when she was one year old.

43A *Aunt Bessie* (1974).
Family of Woman Mask Series.
Acrylic on canvas, fabric, yarn, beads, raffia,
foam base. 65½" x 19" x 12".
Clothing by Willi Posey. Photo: Karen Bell.

43B *Aunt Edith* (1974).
Family of Woman Mask Series.
Acrylic on canvas, fabric, yarn, beads, raffia,
foam base. 64" x 19" x 13".
Clothing by Willi Posey. Photo: Karen Bell.

44 *Martin Luther King* (1975).
Portrait mask.
Acrylic paint, fabric, wig hair, beads, embroidery, foam base.
64" x 33" x 11".
Clothing by Willi Posey. Photo: Karen Bell.

45 *Lena* (1978).
Harlem Series.
Mixed media, 17" tall. Photo: Ron Zak.

46 *Sonny's Quilt* (1986).
Acrylic on canvas, tie-dyed, printed and pieced fabric,
84½" x 60". Collection of Barbara and Ronald Davis Balser,
Atlanta, Georgia. Photo: Gamma I.

47 *The Women: Mask Face Quilt I* (1986).
Acrylic on canvas, tie-dyed, printed and pieced fabric, 69½" x 61".

48 *Dinner Quilt* (1986).
Acrylic on cotton canvas, tie-dyed, printed and pieced fabric,
48½" x 66". Collection of Lynn Plotkin.

50 *Change: Faith Ringgold's Over 100 Pounds Weight Loss Story Quilt*
(1986-1987). Photo etching on silk and cotton canvas, pieced
and printed fabric. 57¼" x 70¼". Collection of Barbara and
Ronald Davis Balser.

Bibliography

Harris, Ann Sutherland and Linda Nochlin. *Women Artists: 1550–1950.*
  New York: Los Angeles County Museum of Art and Alfred A. Knopf, 1977.
Munro, Eleanor. *Originals: American Women Artists.* New York: Simon & Schuster, 1979.
Peterson, Karen, and J.J. Wilson. *Women Artists.* New York: Harper & Row, 1976.
Rubenstein, Charlotte Streifer. *American Women Artists.* New York: Avon Books, 1982.

Georgia O'Keeffe

Castro, Jan. *The Art & Life of Georgia O'Keeffe.* New York: Crown Publishers, 1985.
Cowart, Jack, Sarah Greenough, and Juan Hamilton. *Georgia O'Keeffe: Art and Letters,*
  exhibition catalogue. Washington, D.C.: National Gallery of Art, 1987.
Georgia O'Keeffe: Metropolitan Museum of Art Bulletin. New York: Metropolitan Museum of
  Art, Fall 1984.
Gherman, Beverly. *Georgia O'Keeffe: The "Wideness and Wonder" of Her World.* New York:
  Atheneum, 1986.
Lisle, Laurie. *Portrait of an Artist: A Biography of Georgia O'Keeffe.* New York:
  Washington Square Press, 1986.
O'Keeffe, Georgia. *Georgia O'Keeffe.* New York: The Viking Press, 1976.

Frida Kahlo

Frida Kahlo and Tina Modotti, exhibition catalogue. London: Whitechapel Art Gallery,
  1982.
Herrera, Hayden. *Frida: A Biography of Frida Kahlo.* New York: Harper & Row, 1983.
————. "Frida Kahlo: The Palette, the Pain, and the Painter." *Art Forum,* March 1983.
Lippard, Lucy. "Biofeedback." *The Village Voice,* March 22, 1983.
Newman, Michael. "The Ribbon Around the Bomb." *Art in America,* April 1982.

Alice Neel

Harris, Ann Sutherland. "Alice Neel: 1930–1980." *Alice Neel,* exhibition catalogue.
  Loyola Marymount University Art Gallery, 1983.
Hills, Patricia. *Alice Neel.* New York: Harry N. Abrams, 1983.
————. "Alice Neel: Art as a Form of History." *Alice Neel: Paintings of Two Decades,*
  exhibition catalogue. Boston: Boston University Art Gallery, 1980.

Neel, Alice. "Doctoral Address to Moore College of Art." *Women and Art,* Winter 1971, Vol. 1, no. 1, pp. 12-13.

Nemser, Cindy. "Alice Neel—Teller of Truth." *Alice Neel: The Woman and Her Work,* exhibition catalogue. Athens, Georgia: Georgia Museum of Art, 1975.

———. *Art Talk: Conversations with Twelve Women Artists.* New York: Charles Scribner and Sons, 1975.

Faith Ringgold

Change: Painted Story Quilts, exhibition catalogue. New York: Bernice Steinbaum Gallery, 1987.

Dishman, Laura Stewart. "Ringgold Uses Fabric as a Thread to Her Past." *The Orlando Sentinel,* September 11, 1987, Sec. E, pp. 1 and 3.

———. "Social Message Is Sewn into Sculptures, Quilts." *The Orlando Sentinel,* September 11, 1987, Sec. E, pp. 1 and 3.

Dorsey, John. "Painted 'Quilts' Tell Many Stories at BMA Show." *The Sun,* November 17, 1987, Sec. C, p. 1.

Galligan, Gregory. "The Quilts of Faith Ringgold." *Arts,* January 1987, pp. 62–63.

Gill, Susan. "Faith Ringgold." *Arts,* March 1987, p. 96.

Glueck, Grace. "An Artist Who Turns Cloth into Social Commentary." *New York Times,* July 29, 1984, pp. 24–25.

Gouma-Peterson, Thalia. "Faith Ringgold's Narrative Quilts." *Arts,* January 1987, pp. 64–69.

Lippard, Lucy R. "Faith Ringgold at Bernice Steinbaum." *Art in America,* May 1987, pp. 184–185.

———. "Faith Ringgold's Black, Political Feminist Art." *From the Center.* New York: Dutton, 1976, pp. 257–264.

Sills, Leslie. Interview with Faith Ringgold. New York City, July 1987.

Vespereny, Cynthia. "Faith Ringgold: Storyteller Sews Her Tales." *News-Journal,* October 4, 1987, Sec. H, pp. 1 and 10.

Wallace, Michele. "Baby Faith." *Ms.,* July/August 1987, pp. 154–156, 216.

Leslie Sills says that she was twenty years old before she thought about a career in art. "Growing up in a family of academically oriented people, I thought being an artist, a profession in which one continually uses her hands, was not an option. I thought one had to be *born* an artist."

After graduating with a degree in psychology from Boston University, Leslie worked for a while (unhappily) in a neuropsychology laboratory, studying monkeys. It was by chance that she took a pottery class at a local YWCA and discovered her love of clay. "Could I really spend a lifetime 'playing' in this way?" she asked herself. Inspired by her discovery, she went on to study ceramic sculpture at the School of the Museum of Fine Arts in Boston, Massachusetts, and, while there, began to give art lessons to children. Her interests and talents eventually led her to found and direct the Children's Creative Clay Studio School in Brookline, Massachusetts.

In small classes for children ages five through seventeen, Leslie encouraged her students to independently explore materials and to design their own projects. In addition, she sought to inspire them by taking them on field trips, reading aloud visually exciting stories, projecting slides of famous art works, and mounting juried shows of student art. Through her teaching she soon discovered the shortage of books available about women artists and how little even her most sophisticated students knew about them. This experience and ensuing discussions with her husband, Robert Oresick, a professor of psychology and counseling at Boston University, formed the genesis of *Inspirations: Stories About Women Artists,* along with her desire to show children "that they, too, can play; that being an artist is a viable profession and way of life."

Leslie Sills' sculpture, a mix of fantasy and realism with feminist themes, has been exhibited in galleries and museums throughout the Northeast. She has also lectured and published articles on art and art education.

At present, she lives in Brookline, Massachusetts, with her husband and young son, Eric.